W9-CNL-896

Better Homes and Gardens®

WILDFLOWERS
AND
SPECIAL GARDENS

Excerpted from Better Homes and Gardens® *COMPLETE GUIDE TO GARDENING*

CONTENTS

EVERY GARDEN CAN BE SPECIAL

Whether surroundings dictate it or we just dare to be different, many of us want our gardens to go beyond a simple arrangement of flower beds. We want them to be *special.* Your definition of special may be a formal sitting area. Or, it may be a more natural setting like the one at left. You may prefer to take a walk on color's wild side by strolling through a meadow of wildflowers. Or, if your dining tastes lean toward the fresh and natural, you may want your garden to include a potpourri of herbs. But, whatever your gardening needs, this book offers a variety of special ways to satisfy them.

Commercial wildflower seed mixes are tailored to specific regions. Usually, they contain seeds of native flowers and species that adapt to almost any climate.

Wildflowers

Awakening as the soil warms, wildflowers announce the arrival of a new season. Enjoy their beauty from early spring to autumn.

The secret of a successful wildflower garden is working with nature to select the correct plants for your environment. Choose several kinds of flowers so you have blooms all summer and in autumn, besides early spring. Include foliage plants that will complement the flowers and berries, and add a variety of shapes and textures. Ferns work well in shady, moist areas. Mayapple and jack-in-the-pulpit make interesting ground covers.

Wildflowers are often split into two groups—sun lovers and shade lovers. Almost all of the spring-blooming species will adapt to an area receiving filtered light.

Buy wildflower roots or bulbs from a nursery or catalogue to avoid endangering rare species. Or, get wildflower starts from friends. Wildflower hobbyists usually will share extras when they divide their plantings—especially if you'll trade for part of one of your favorites. Otherwise, take only from a construction site or a condemned property. If you gather roadside seeds, don't take them all from one area—leave some to flower next year.

Propagate your own plants, raising them from cuttings or seeds. Set out spring-blooming wildflowers in the autumn, and summer- and fall-blooming plants in the summer or fall. For best effect, avoid rows.

Select plants that will do well in the environment you have, or change the environment to meet the plants' needs. To know what plants will flourish on your property, study your area's characteristics. Find out what grew originally on your property. Also study the slope of the land, the prevailing winds, the aver-

age amount of rainfall per year, the level of humidity, and the water drainage patterns. After analyzing each, you'll have a good idea of the wildflowers able to grow in your yard. Study existing vegetation, too.

If you must change the environment to grow the wildflowers you want, create the right conditions—shade, soil, and moisture—before you purchase your plants. The closer you come to creating the conditions the plants prefer when growing naturally, the better they will do. The amount of sunlight and wind is controlled by trees and shrubs, for example.

Moisture depends on rainfall, surface contours, and soil type. It may be necessary to water wildflowers native to moist habitats more often than you water other plants.

The soil structure and chemical composition often dictate what plants will flourish. Usually, you won't need special soils; a typical garden loam is fine for all wildflowers but desert species.

Wildflowers won't grow in close-packed or compacted soil, however, because their roots will suffocate. Add leaf mold to compacted soil to loosen it. Another way to keep soil loose is to establish paths of wood

chips or gravel in your garden. Then, foot traffic won't pack the soil around the plants.

After your garden is planted, do not cultivate with a hoe; instead, do all the weeding by hand. Cover the bare earth around the plants with a leaf mulch until existing vegetation takes over. Don't use a chemical fertilizer or a weed killer on your wildflower garden.

As the growing season comes to an end, protect the plants against winter with a four- to five-inch layer of leaves. Remove the leaves in spring after the danger of frost passes; a few may be left to rot.

Wildflowers can turn a grassy expanse into a lush, colorful carpet that puts an end to uphill mowing chores.

Wild-flowers in Sunny Spots

Carpet a corner with sun-loving wildflowers and you'll be rewarded with a pageant of color as one species after another comes to bloom. To ensure a good stand, sow new seed yearly.

Sow packaged mixed wildflower seeds from a commercial grower for a variety of continuous blooms all summer long. You'll find you can transform an everyday lawn into a blossoming meadow with wild-flowers, and you can retire your lawn mower, too.

California poppies (*Eschscholzia*) open when the sun strikes them and close when the sun sets. The bright yellow to deep orange blooms are offset by feathery blue-green foliage.

Butterfly weed (*Asclepias*) will catch the attention of butterflies and is a good candidate for meadows. On a smaller scale, it mixes well with non-native annuals and perennials in a flower border. This plant thrives in sunny, dry places.

Purple coneflowers (*Echinacea*) have stiff branching stems with solitary flowers. The flowers resemble black-eyed susans in shape, except that the petals curve backward. The three- to four-inch purple-red flowers have a prickly, rising dome for the flower head.

Forget-me-nots (*Myosotis*) are praised throughout poetry and folklore. They grow well at the edge of a brook or pool and in other moist locations, and are a pale blue.

Marsh marigolds (*Caltha*), too, like it damp. They grow best along the banks of streams or, as their name implies, in swampy areas.

Living up to its name, the brilliant orange butterfly weed attracts a host of colorful insects.

The well-known black-eyed susan spreads quickly.

Queen-Anne's-lace takes over with no care from you.

Create a meadow of wildflowers to bloom next spring in your own yard—whether it's a wide-open space as above or a tiny urban backyard!

Wildflowers in the Shade

Many wildflowers grow prettily in shady places similar to their woodland homes. They can be problem-solvers, too, by occupying spots where few other plants thrive.

Dutchman's-breeches and hepaticas claim this shady nook with their fancy foliage. They're tiny but breathtaking.

Although not spectacular in size and color, wildflowers for shady spots deserve a close look. Their subtlety is their charm.

Trillium blooms in spring with a three-petaled, waxy flower measuring about two inches across. Start it in soil rich in organic matter. Trillium is perfect with other low-light favorites, such as hostas or violets.

Snakeroot (*Cimicifuga*) is best at the back of your garden because it often grows to eight feet tall.

Hepatica, named for its liver-shaped leaves, blooms on the first warm days. Hepaticas like to be planted in woodsy settings but need some sun while blossoming.

Bloodroot (*Sanguinaria*) will spread quickly into clumps. Blooms are white; sap is bloodred.

Dutchman's-breeches (*Dicentra*) have three to 12 white flowers that look like wide "breeches" on each plant. The plant prefers a rich, woods-like soil.

To add decorative foliage, try ferns. Most grow best in the shade. Depending on the variety, ferns will grow under either semi-dry or moist conditions.

Maidenhair fern (*Adiantum*) prefers a mulched, woodsy soil. This fern will spread gradually as a filler between other shady plants.

Ostrich fern (*Matteuccia*), if planted along the banks of a stream or in a wet, marshy spot, will help control erosion.

The hardy jack-in-the-pulpit likes sheltered, shady spots.

Trillium will sport berries after flowering.

This summer show of royal fern, bluet, mayapple, bleeding-heart, Virginia bluebell, and wild geraniums is happiest when left completely undisturbed.

Love and effort restored this woodland. The landowners cleared small areas at a time, then planted native wildflowers, shrubs, and trees.

WILDFLOWERS

Name	Description	Soil and Light	Propagation	Comments
ALUMROOT *Heuchera*	Tiny blossoms on stems 16 to 36 inches tall. White, red, purplish. Blooms from May to August.	Shady location. Well-drained, dry soil.	Seeds or division.	Leaves mottled when young.
ANEMONE, RUE *Anemonella*	Delicate blossoms on stems 5 to 9 inches tall. White and pink. Blooms from March to June.	Shady location. Well-drained, dry soil.	Seeds or division.	Divide after plant has died back in the fall.
ARBUTUS, TRAILING *Epigaea*	Tubular white and pink blossoms from March to May. Plants are 3 inches high.	Partial shade. Well-drained, dry soil.	Seeds, stem cuttings, or stem layering.	Keep well mulched. Bears white berries.
BANEBERRY *Actaea*	Small, white blossoms in April and May. Later, red or white berries on 2-foot high plants.	Shade. Well-drained, dry soil.	Seeds or division.	Sow seeds in the fall.
BEE BALM *Monarda*	Large, red blossoms on 2-foot high plants from June to September.	Shade. Well-drained, moist, acid soil.	Seeds, stem cuttings, or division.	Will adapt to partially sunny location.
BELLWORT *Uvularia*	Pale yellow blossoms on graceful 4- to 12-inch plants from April to June.	Shade. Well-drained, moist soil.	Seeds or division.	Fleshy, winged seed capsules.
BISHOP'S-CAP *Mitella*	Tiny, white flowers from April to June on 6- to 12-inch plants.	Shade. Well-drained, moist soil.	Seeds or division.	Keep well mulched.
BLACK-EYED SUSAN *Rudbeckia hirta*	Flat, daisy-like flowers on 2-foot high wiry stems; yellow petals with brown centers. Blooms in July and August.	Sunny. Well-drained soil.	Seeds, but often self-sows.	Often grown as biennial.
BLOODROOT *Sanguinaria*	Large leaved, with single white flowers in April and May on plants 8 to 10 inches high.	Shade. Well-drained, dry soil.	Seeds or division.	One leaf for each flower. Leaves form thick mat.
BLUEBELLS *Mertensia*	Two-foot tall stems with blue flowers in April and May.	Sun or partial shade. Well-drained, moist soil.	Seeds or division.	Plants disappear during the summer.
BUTTERCUP **Crowfoot** *Ranunculus*	Small, yellow flowers from April to August on plants 6 to 24 inches high.	Shade or partial shade. Tolerant of most soil types.	Seeds or division.	Can become like a weed.
BUTTERFLY WEED *Asclepias tuberosa*	Clusters of small, red-orange flowers in July and August on plants 2 feet high.	Sunny. Well-drained, dry soil.	Seeds or root cuttings.	Brilliant color.
CARDINAL FLOWER *Lobelia cardinalis*	Clusters of tubular, red flowers from July to September on plants 2 to 3 feet tall.	Partial shade. Well-drained, moist, acid soil.	Offsets, divisions, stem cuttings, or seeds; often self-sows.	Keep well mulched.
CINQUEFOIL *Potentilla*	Tiny, yellow flowers from June to August on 3- to 6-inch plants that turn red in fall.	Shade. Well-drained, dry, acid soil.	Seeds, division, or stem cuttings.	Good ground cover.

WILDFLOWERS (continued)

Name	Description	Soil and Light	Propagation	Comments
COLUMBINE, WILD *Aquilegia*	Finely cut, pendulous, yellow and red flowers from April through July on 1- to 2-foot plants.	Shade. Well-drained, dry, slightly acid soil.	Seeds, but often self-sows.	Showy.
CONEFLOWER, PRAIRIE *Ratibida*	Large, yellow flowers from June to August on plants up to 6 feet tall.	Sunny. Well-drained, dry soil.	Seeds or division.	Graceful and showy.
CONEFLOWER, PURPLE *Echinacea*	Large, single, purple flowers from June to October on plants 3 to 4 feet tall.	Sunny. Well-drained, dry soil.	Seeds or division.	Tall and impressive.
DOG-TOOTH VIOLET Adder's-tongue, Trout lily *Erythronium*	Solitary white flowers in April and May on plants 6 inches tall.	Shade. Well-drained, moist soil.	Offsets or seeds.	Forms a dense mat. Leaves are mottled with brown.
DUTCHMAN'S-BREECHES *Dicentra cucullaria*	Unusually shaped, white flowers in April and May, clustered on stems of plants 6 to 12 inches high.	Shade. Well-drained, dry soil.	Division or seeds.	Spreads into clumps. Disappears after flowering.
EVENING PRIMROSE *Oenothera*	Pale yellow, fragrant flowers in July and August on plants 2 to 4 feet tall.	Sunny. Well drained, dry soil.	Seeds.	Flowers open only at night. Treat as a biennial.
FLAG, BLUE *Iris sp.*	Large, purple blossoms in May and June on plants 2 to 3 feet tall.	Sunny. Moist to wet, slightly acid soil.	Division or seeds, but often self-sows.	Forms a dense colony.
FOAMFLOWER False miterwort *Tiarella*	Small, white flowers cluster on plants 6 to 12 inches high.	Shade. Well-drained, moist soil.	Division or seeds.	Effective in mass.
FORGET-ME-NOT *Myosotis*	Pale blue flowers with yellow centers on 6-inch plants. Blooms all summer long if conditions are right.	Sunny. Well-drained, moist to wet soil.	Division or seeds.	Keep moist.
GENTIAN, CLOSED Blue gentian *Gentiana andrewsi*	Tubular, violet flowers in August and September on plants 1 foot tall.	Sun or partial shade. Well-drained, moist to wet, slightly acid soil.	Division or seeds.	Flowers remain closed.
GERANIUM, WILD *Geranium maculatum*	Large, red-violet flowers in clusters on plants 2 feet tall.	Shade. Well-drained, moist soil.	Division or seeds.	Effective in mass.
GINGER, WILD *Asarum*	Inconspicuous, tubular, violet-brown flowers in April and May. Blooms appear at the base of plants that will grow to 4 to 8 inches tall.	Shade. Well-drained, moist soil.	Division or rhizome cuttings.	Interesting ground cover.
HEPATICA *Hepatica*	Rose, white, or blue flowers from April to May on 6-inch plants.	Shade. Well-drained, dry, slightly acid soil.	Division or seeds, but often self-sows.	Valued for early color. Showy.

Name	Description	Soil and Light	Propagation	Comments
JACK-IN-THE-PULPIT *Arisaema triphyllum*	Unusual, vase-shaped, greenish-brown flowers from April to June on plants 2 feet tall. Red berries follow later in the season.	Shade. Well-drained, moist soil.	Seeds, but often self-sows.	Showy and attractive.
JACOB'S-LADDER Greek valerian *Polemonium*	Small clusters of blue flowers on 3-foot plants in June and July.	Shade. Well-drained, moist soil.	Division or seeds.	Fine border plant.
LADY-SLIPPER, YELLOW *Cypripedium calceolus*	Yellow flowers (often veined in blue) bloom in May on plants to 30 inches tall.	Shade. Well-drained, moist soil.	Division.	Showy. Give an annual topdressing of compost.
LOBELIA, BLUE *Lobelia siphilitica*	Tiny, blue flowers from August to October on terminal clusters of plants 2 to 3 feet tall.	Sun or partial shade. Well-drained, moist soil.	Division, offsets, stem cuttings, or seeds.	Valuable for late summer color.
MALLOW, ROSE *Hibiscus*	Large, red, pink, or white flowers from July to September on plants 6 feet tall.	Sunny. Well-drained, moist soil.	Division, stem cuttings, or seeds.	Use as a background plant.
MARIGOLD, MARSH *Caltha*	Small clusters of brilliant yellow flowers in April and May on plants 2 feet tall.	Sunny. Moist to wet soil.	Division.	Plants disappear in summer.
MAYAPPLE Mandrake *Podophyllum*	Single, white, daisy-like flower in April and May on 12- to 18-inch plants.	Partial to full shade. Well-drained, moist soil.	Division or seeds.	Rapid spreader. Good, quick ground cover.
MEADOW RUE, EARLY *Thalictrum dioicum*	Inconspicuous, greenish or violet flowers in April and May on 2-foot plants.	Shade. Well-drained, moist soil.	Division or seeds.	Handsome, dainty foliage.
MEADOW RUE, TALL *Thalictrum polygamum*	Large clusters of white flowers from August to September on plants to 10 feet tall.	Sunny. Well-drained, moist to wet soil.	Division, stem cuttings, or seeds.	Use as background plant.
PARTRIDGEBERRY *Mitchella*	Small, white flowers in June and July on plants to 6 inches tall. Small red berries follow later in the season.	Shade. Well-drained, moist, acid soil	Stem cuttings or seeds.	Effective ground cover.
PASQUEFLOWER *Anemone sp.*	Large, purple flowers in March and April on plants 16 inches tall.	Sunny. Well-drained, dry soil.	Seeds or root cuttings.	Early and attractive.
PHLOX, BLUE *Phlox divaricata*	Clusters of pale blue flowers in April and May on stems 6 to 15 inches tall. Small leaves appear opposite each other on the stem.	Partial shade. Well-drained, dry soil.	Division or stem cuttings.	Often forms large clumps.
POPPY, CALIFORNIA *Eschscholzia*	Brilliant orange, cuplike flowers from April to June on plants 10 to 20 inches tall.	Sunny. Well-drained, dry soil.	Seeds.	Vigorous and hardy.

WILDFLOWERS (continued)

Name	Description	Soil and Light	Propagation	Comments
PRAIRIE ROSE *Rosa setigera*	Pink flowers from May to July in small clusters. Branches grow up to 15 feet long.	Sunny. Well-drained, dry soil.	Seeds or stem layering.	Branches are thornless.
SAND VERBENA *Abronia*	Small, pink, yellow, or lilac flowers from May to September on low plants.	Sunny. Well-drained, dry soil.	Seeds.	Trailing stems creep along the ground.
SHOOTING-STAR *Dodecatheon*	Small, attractive, red-violet flowers in May and June in clusters on foot-long stalks.	Light shade. Well-drained, moist soil.	Division, root cuttings, or seeds.	Plant disappears in summer.
SNAKEROOT *Cimicifuga*	Tiny, white blossoms in spike clusters from July to September on plants up to 8 feet tall.	Shade. Well-drained, moist soil.	Division or seeds.	Dried plants work well in fall arrangements.
SOLOMON'S-SEAL *Polygonatum*	Inconspicuous, greenish-white, bell-shaped flowers appear in May and June under the leaves on plants 1 to 2 feet tall. Bluish-black berries follow.	Shade. Well-drained, dry, slightly acid soil.	Division or seeds, but often self-sows.	Good ground cover in shady areas.
SPIDERWORT *Tradescantia*	Blue or white flowers in small terminal clusters on 1 to 2 foot, grasslike plants. Has blooms from June to August.	Sun or partial shade. Well-drained, moist soil.	Division, stem cuttings, or seeds.	Vigorous and quick growing.
SPRING-BEAUTY *Claytonia*	Delicate, pinkish-white blossoms from March to May on plants 4 to 6 inches tall.	Shade. Well-drained, dry soil.	Division or seeds, but often self-sows.	Good ground cover in shady areas.
SUNFLOWER, SAWTOOTH *Helianthus giganteus*	Large, yellow blossoms with brown centers in clusters on plants 10 feet tall. Has flowers from July to October.	Sunny. Well-drained soil.	Division or seeds.	Showy background plant.
TOOTHWORT *Dentaria*	Tiny, pinkish-white flowers in April and May in small clusters on plants 6 to 12 inches tall.	Shade. Well-drained, moist soil.	Division or seeds.	Valued for early spring color.
TRILLIUM *Trillium*	White or purple blossoms from April to June. The erect stems are about a foot long.	Shade. Well-drained, moist soil.	Division or seeds.	Effective in mass. Showy.
TURTLEHEAD *Chelone*	White or pink flowers line stem like snapdragons from July to September on plants 3 feet tall.	Shade. Well-drained, moist soil.	Division, stem cuttings, or seeds.	Interesting and handsome.
VIOLET *Viola sp.*	Flowers from April to June on small 6- to 8-inch plants.	Shade. Well-drained, moist soil.	Division or seeds, but often self-sows.	Can become like a weed.
WOOD ASTER, BLUE *Aster cordifolius*	Small, light purple flowers that bloom as open clusters in August and September. Plants grow up to 4 feet tall.	Partial to full shade. Well-drained, moist soil.	Division.	Good background plants.
WOOD ASTER, WHITE *Aster divaricatus*	Small, whitish-purple blossoms appear in flat clusters on 15-inch plants in August and September.	Partial shade. Well-drained, moist soil.	Division, but often self-sows.	Effective in mass. Vigorous and attractive.

FERNS

Name	Height in Inches	Soil and Light	Comments
Beech *Thelypteris hexagonoptera*	8-16	Shade. Well-drained, dry soil.	Striking, triangular leaves that are wider than they are long. Easy to grow, forming a dense mat.
Bracken *Pteridium*	16-32	Shade. Well-drained, moist or dry soil.	Large, coarse fern. Good for background planting.
Christmas *Polystichum acrostichoides*	12-30	Shade. Well-drained, moist soil.	Excellent for cutting. Can take some sun.
Cinnamon *Osmunda cinnamomea*	30-60	Shade. Well-drained, damp, acid soil.	Eight-inch-wide fronds turn to a cinnamon brown.
Ground cedar *Lycopodium sp.*	2-4	Shade. Well-drained, dry soil.	Dainty and fernlike. Good for poor, open forest soils.
Ground pine *Lycopodium sp.*	5-8	Shade. Well-drained, dry soil.	Looks like small tree. Not really a fern but is similar.
Hay-scented *Dennstaedtia punctilobula*	16-36	Shade. Tolerant of most well-drained soil conditions.	Lacelike fronds. Quick-spreading ground cover; useful on slopes.
Interrupted *Osmunda claytoniana*	24-48	Shade. Well-drained, damp, acid soil.	Graceful, large fronds in clusters. Grows slowly.
Lady, Northern *Athyrium filix-femina*	16-32	Shade. Well-drained, dry soil.	Finely toothed fronds.
Maidenhair *Adiantum*	10-20	Shade. Well-drained, moist soil.	Lacy fronds on black, wiry stems.
Male *Dryopteris filix-mas*	12-30	Shade. Well-drained, moist, gravelly soil.	Try them massed under trees.
New York *Thelypteris noveboracensis*	12-24	Shade. Well-drained, dry, slightly acid soil.	Quick-spreading ground cover. Formerly called *Dryopteris noveboracensis*.
Ostrich *Matteuccia*	24-60	Shade. Well-drained, moist to wet soil.	One of the tallest and most stately ferns. Plume-like fronds. Use in backgrounds.
Polypody *Polypodium*	4-36	Open shade. Well-drained, dry, gravelly soil.	Forms great mats over rocks and steep banks. Evergreen.
Rattlesnake *Botrychium virginianum*	8-24	Shade. Well-drained, moist soil.	Dainty fronds. Attracts snails.
Royal *Osmunda regalis*	Up to 72	Open shade. Well-drained, moist to wet, acid soil.	Tall, dramatic clumps.
Sensitive *Onoclea sensibilis*	24-54	Open shade to partial sun. Well-drained, moist to wet soil.	Handsome, showy fern. Delicate, bronzy-pink foliage.
Spleenwort, Ebony *Asplenium platyneuron*	6-15	Shade. Well-drained, dry soil.	Extremely hardy evergreen species. Plant between rocks.
Spleenwort, Maidenhair *Asplenium trichomanes*	3-6	Shade. Well-drained, dry soil mixed with limestone chips.	Will thrive in any rock cleft, if given foothold.
Walking *Camptosorus rhizophyllus*	4-12	Shade. Well-drained, dry soil.	Delicate. Best suited to rock garden. Reproduces from leaf tips. Attracts slugs.
Wood, Evergreen *Dryopteris sp.*	12-24	Shade. Well-drained, dry soil.	Deep green, thick fronds.

Annuals make great sow-and-grow cutting gardens. They sprout quickly from seed and produce a bumper crop of blossoms.

Flowers for Cutting

The beauty of a main border can be marred by snipping flowers for floral arrangements and bouquets. But both a beautiful border and a house full of flowers are possible by growing a cutting garden.

A cutting garden is a plot of land set aside for the purpose of growing flowers for indoor bouquets only. If well planned, this garden will supply cut flowers for floral arrangements from early spring through late fall.

Grow a cutting garden in a sunny—but secluded—spot. Such a specialty is not grown for beauty outdoors but for the beauty of indoor arrangements. For example, set it behind a border, where the coming and going of blooms will go unnoticed. Or plant it in your vegetable garden because the culture of many glorious annuals is similar to that of vegetables.

Include perennials, biennials, and annuals in your cutting garden, but set the perennials apart from the biennials and annuals so the perennials' root systems will be undisturbed. For a succession of blooms, plant short-season annuals and tender bulbs every three weeks. And select varieties that bloom at different times.

A popular way to grow flowers for a cutting garden is in rows. Developing to perfection, the flowers may be picked often without a thought of causing gaps in a more visible border.

To make access to flowers easier, make a path through the garden. A path can be just bare earth you walk on to pack down. This is simple to dig up if the garden is to be used later for another purpose. Or lay concrete slabs; they can be removed at the end of each season.

Still easier is to make the garden small enough that paths are unnecessary because the flowers can be reached easily for cutting. That way, you can turn even the smallest spot in your yard into a cutting garden.

Little work is one of the charms of the cutting garden: prepare the soil, plant the garden, and keep control of the weeds.

But be sure to prepare the soil well. Each year in the fall, add a compost mixture to the soil, and spade it in so the ground will be easier to work in the spring.

Hoe the garden throughout the growing season to control weeds. Or, after the flowers have sprouted, add mulch to keep weeds down.

There's no need to remove yellowing foliage from plants; the garden's only purpose is to raise cut flowers, not provide beauty outdoors. But you may want to remove the flower heads after they fade to prolong the flowering period. That way the plant will not waste energy on flowers past the right stage for displaying. Picking the spent flower heads will encourage the plant to produce another crop of blooms.

With extra planning, it's possible to grow two cutting gardens on the same plot of land within a year's time.

In fall, plant a spring cutting garden; months later it is fresh with spring-blooming tulips and daffodils in a painter's palette full of colors. Later, you might dig up the bulbs and plant a summer cutting garden, complete with annuals blooming into autumn. Mingle vegetable plants among the flowering plants.

For year-after-year blooms, plant perennials in a spot all their own.

Tulips and daffodils grow profusely every spring if planted correctly. Plant the bulbs in good garden loam with thorough drainage. In the fall, work the soil and enrich with organic matter before planting the bulbs. For best effect indoors, be sure to choose varieties that will complement the colors of your decor.

After the plants are through blooming, the foliage will turn yellow and die back.

If you've decided to go to the extra effort of planting a summer garden in the same spot, the spring-flowering bulbs will have to be dug up before all of the foliage has died back. However, this aging process is necessary for the strength of next year's bulbs. Dig a trench in another area and place the maturing tulip and daffodil bulbs there—dug intact with foliage—so the plants will die back naturally, completing the process of storing nutrients.

Include several different classes of tulips in a spring cutting garden. Early double and early single tulips both flower in April in most parts of the country. Triumph and mendel tulips are mid-season bloomers. Darwin, lily-flowered, and cottage tulips all bloom about a month later. Choose varieties and colors in each of these classes that will complement one another in an arrangement for the table or sideboard. Twenty bulbs of each variety will give a good yield of spring flowers.

For a sunny display of daffodils, plant double narcissus, large-cupped narcissus, bicolor trumpets, yellow trumpets, pink daffodils, and white trumpets. With the help of a good bulb catalogue, choose varieties that bloom at different times throughout the spring.

PLANTING TIPS

Use bonemeal to define garden mini-beds. Sow seeds inside the beds.

Lightly cover the seeds with compost, peat moss, or potting soil. Tamp gently.

Label each bed and water thoroughly. Keep slightly moist at all times.

A bouquet of cut flowers creates floral artistry.

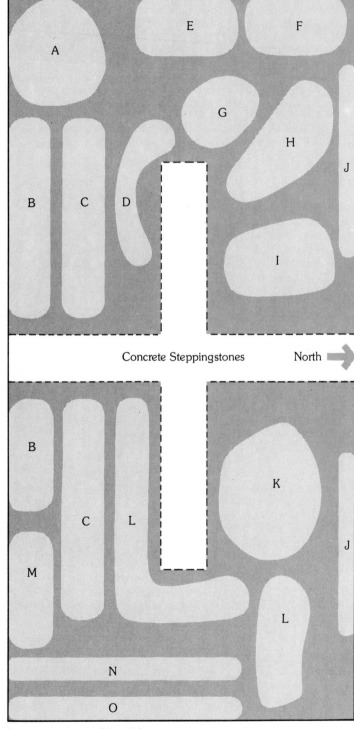

Concrete Steppingstones North →

Summer cutting garden 7 ft. x 14 ft.

A. Zucchini
B. Geranium
C. Chrysanthemum
D. Scabiosa
E. Ammobium

F. Pepper
G. Xeranthemum
H. Marigold
I. Statice
J. Nasturtium on trellis

K. Tetra zinnia
L. Dwarf dahlia
M. Telstar petunia
N. Beet
O. Carrot

Gain privacy and harvest cut flowers with a tall hedge of pink cleome.

Summer Cutting Garden

As spring warms into summer, plant a cutting garden with summer- and autumn-blooming beauties. Choose from the many kinds of annuals available today. Select plants that will flower at different times during the seasons.

Because the planting and culture of annuals are similar to those of vegetables, several kinds of vegetables also can be grown in your cutting garden. Peppers, zucchini, beets, and carrots will all grow well. Or, plant your cutting garden in the vegetable garden and eliminate preparing a separate plot of land.

Flowers bloom much sooner when seedlings are set out, rather than when seeds are sown directly into the garden. Start your own plants in early spring by sowing seeds indoors in a flat. Or purchase bedding plants from a good garden center. Dwarf dahlias and petunias should be sown in seedbeds or flats in early spring for a May planting date in the cutting garden. Plant only sturdy, healthy seedlings for best results.

The summer garden (at left) is plotted creatively. (Straight rows work as well.) The path is optional and is made of concrete steppingstones so the annuals can be easily reached for cutting or weeding.

Many annuals make excellent dried flowers for fall arrangements. Dried statice, xeranthemum, and ammobium will make long-lasting bouquets.

Cut flowers add elegance to dining.

Handling Cut Flowers

Delight a friend and please the family with flowers from your garden. Whether an artistically planned arrangement or a simple, single bloom in a bud vase, flowers brighten any room.

A little know-how about handling cut flowers will keep them glowing in a fresh floral arrangement. Flowers remain alive after cutting, so they need proper treatment and care to help them take up and retain water. They need a constant water supply to transport food and to keep the stems stiff.

Gathering freshly cut flowers in a basket may sound lovely, but if you handle cut flowers this way, they will lose water quickly and wilt. As a result, the flowers will have a short life. To gather flowers correctly, carry a pail of tepid water to the garden. Use lukewarm water, not cool, because the plants are stimulated by warmth and slowed by coolness.

Heliotrope

Cut flower stems at an angle and plunge them into the pail of water, deep enough to almost reach the flower heads. If putting several kinds of blooms in one pail, wrap each kind in sheets of newspaper first to keep them separated from one another.

If you're cutting only a few stems and bringing them indoors immediately, it isn't necessary to carry water with you to the garden. Instead, cut the stems and carry the flowers with their heads down. This will keep the stems straight and prevent the flower heads from breaking off.

Resnip each stem at an angle underwater before placing the stems in a pail of tepid water. Place the pail in a cool spot out of direct sunlight, and let stand until the water reaches room temperature. This may take several hours or even overnight. This step, which should be done be-

Sanvitalia

fore arranging the flowers, is known as conditioning.

It is best to pick flowers in the early morning or the late evening, when the temperature is coolest. Also, avoid flowers that have been damaged by insects, diseases, or weather. Marred flowers will only detract from the beauty of your flower arrangement.

To add to the good looks and life of your bouquet, be careful to pick flowers that are at the perfect stage for cutting. Avoid buds that are too tight; they will never fully open. Also avoid flowers that are at full bloom because their life expectancy after picking will be short. Flowers that bloom in clusters should be cut when half of the blooms are open.

For stems that are thick or woody, make a one- to two-inch slit with scissors or a sharp knife from the base of the stem upward. This will help the stem take in enough water for the blooms to keep supplied with moisture. Otherwise, moisture will be unavailable and the

flowers and foliage will wilt even more quickly.

Poppies, dahlias, and other garden flowers with hollow stems (or stems that secrete a milky substance when cut) need to be seared with a flame immediately after cutting. The burner from your chafing dish will do nicely. A candle works just as well, however.

Carry the candle or other means of producing a flame with you into the garden, and sear stems as you go. If the stems are recut when arranging the flowers, resear them.

Flowers whose stems have been seared still need to be conditioned. Plunge them into a pail of lukewarm water and leave them there for several hours or overnight.

After tulips and roses are picked, their buds and flowers open in a hurry. To slow the process, gently hold the blooms shut with florist's tape until the fresh arrangement is put on display.

Always use clean containers for floral arrangements. Clip off all foliage that will be under the water level in the finished arrangement. Leaves in the water disintegrate rapidly, give the water a foul smell, and shorten the life of cut flowers.

Heavy-headed flowers, such as large mums, often bend by the flower heads. To temporarily improve the situation, insert a toothpick pointed at both ends through the bloom into the stem to add support. Such blooms are not long lasting.

If you want to use garden lilies in a centerpiece, snip off the pollen-

Tithonia

bearing stems of each bloom before you make the arrangement. Otherwise, bits of stamen are apt to drop off and stain the flowers—and the tablecloth below. These stains are hard to remove.

Cleome

Fully opened chrysanthemums help make floral arrangements beautiful, but their petals drop off easily. To keep the petals on, hold the stems upside down and drip candle wax carefully around the calyx. The calyx is the outer circle of green under the petals.

In combining flowers, you'll find an arrangement is most effective when it has been designed to suit a specific setting. The size, shape, and color of a flower composition should fit into its surroundings and be displayed in a container complementing both flowers and decor.

On a small table, a dainty arrangement is both attention-getting and appealing. A tall vase requires height in the arrangement, and a shallow bowl will display a short flower arrangement well.

Coordinating the colors of flowers to colors of room furnishings makes both look better. Yellow snapdragons and mums, for example, will pick up the yellows, golds, and similar shades in upholstery.

Place your finished floral arrangement away from drafts. Air circulating from air conditioners or fans will soon dry out the flowers. Keep them out of direct sunlight, too, as this will cause dehydration and the flowers will wilt soon.

Dried Flowers

As winter whistles around corners and paints the landscape gray, you can have a souvenir of summer with a bright or subdued arrangement of dried flowers—many grown in your own garden. Some keep a sweet scent.

Unlike your favorite snip-and-display fresh flowers, a dried arrangement is a longer project.

Collect and dry flowers during the summer and fall. Gather blooms from flower gardens, herb gardens, ditches, roadsides, and creek banks. By winter, you'll have a supply of preserved materials.

Use any of several drying methods—all are easy. Select the method that best suits you: silica gel, borax, air drying, pressing, or glycerin.

Pick healthy flowers at various stages of development. This adds a natural look to your arrangements.

Silica gel

Using silica gel to dry flowers is called desiccant drying. A desiccant absorbs moisture, and, with flowers, the silica gel takes moisture from the plants.

Actually, silica gel isn't a gel at all, just tiny blue crystals. It is available at craft stores and is reusable. (To reuse, simply heat it for one hour in a 250 degree Fahrenheit oven. This will restore the crystals to full potency.)

A metal container with a tight lid, such as a cookie tin or a coffee can, is needed for this technique. Put one to two inches of silica gel in the bottom of the container. Place the flowers, with their stems cut to about one inch, face up in the drying medium. Do not let flower petals touch or overlap. Gently sprinkle another inch of the silica gel crystals over the flowers in the container.

Place the cover tightly on the tin, and put the container in a dark, dry place for the required amount of time (see chart, opposite page). When the flowers are dry, the petals should feel papery and brittle.

To remove the flowers from the container, slowly pour off the silica gel, while cupping your hand under the flower head. Gently shake off the drying compound, and remove any excess granules with a soft artist's brush.

When drying delphiniums, larkspur, rosebuds, other buds, snapdragons, lilacs, and leaves, lay them in a horizontal position in the silica gel.

For flowers that work well in silica gel, see the chart. Dark red flowers turn black in the process. Other colors are preserved beautifully.

A dark, dry attic is perfect for drying—and storing—flowers that will become part of a pretty bouquet.

Store the dried flowers in airtight boxes, such as plastic shoe boxes, until ready for use. To keep the flowers in good condition, place the stems in dry floral foam. This will keep them from being damaged. To keep dried plant material in top condition, especially over prolonged periods or when excessive humidity may be a problem, add three or four tablespoons of silica gel to the storage container.

A petal that has fallen from a flower can be repaired easily. Place a dab of white glue on the end of the petal, and rejoin the petal to the flower center using a pair of tweezers.

Borax

Use ordinary household borax in the same manner as silica gel. Directions are the same, except the flower should be placed face down, and the lid should be left off while the flowers dry. Borax is a less expensive method than silica gel, but it takes twice the amount of time. Also, borax doesn't preserve flower color quite as well.

Air drying

Air drying is easy. Start by gathering flowers at midday when blooms are at their best. Don't pick flowers after a heavy rain or when they're covered with dew, because mildew can form and cause the flowers to rot.

Strip all leaves and foliage from the stems. Gather the stems together in a bunch and bind with elastic ties. Hang the bunches of flowers upside down in a dark, dry, well-ventilated room. The air drying process takes two to three weeks.

Pressing

A thick telephone book is perfect for pressing flowers. At one-inch intervals throughout the book, place a layer of newspaper with a layer of facial tissue on top. Put a flower on the facial tissue, and cover with another layer of facial tissue and newspaper. If the facial tissue is omitted, the ink from the newspaper or phone book may be picked up by the flowers. Use the same thickness of materials on each page

DRIED FLOWER AND FOLIAGE TIME CHART

Drying Method	Time	Plants
Silica gel	2 to 3 days	Coralbells, lantana, miniature rose, myosotis, viola
	3 to 4 days	Dwarf dahlia, dwarf marigold, feverfew, larkspur, pansy, small zinnia, tea rose
	4 to 5 days	Buttercup, delphinium, hydrangea, large zinnia, peony, shasta daisy
	5 to 6 days	Aster, calendula, large dahlia, lilac, marigold, snapdragon
Borax	Double above drying times	Any recommended for silica gel
Pressing	3 to 4 weeks	Buttercup, daisy, delphinium, dusty-miller, fern, hydrangea florets, lobelia, pansy, sweet alyssum, verbena, viola
Air drying	2 to 3 weeks	Annual statice, artemisia, bells-of-Ireland, blue salvia, celosia, Chinese-lantern, delphinium, glove amaranth, heather, honesty, larkspur, peegee hydrangea, strawflower, yarrow
		Field flowers: dock, goldenrod, pampas grass, teasel, tansy
Glycerin	1 to 2 weeks	Foliage: aspidistra, beech, crab apple, eucalyptus, holly, laurel, oak, peony, pyracantha, sycamore, yew

for even drying. With a weight (more books or a brick, perhaps) on the telephone book, store for three to four weeks in a dark, dry place.

The flattened flowers won't make three-dimensional arrangements but can be used to make a picture. Buds, stems, and leaves also can be pressed to complete an attractive picture. Use tweezers and white glue to anchor the flowers to the background material. Let the picture dry overnight. Then insert it in a frame and cover with glass. Tape the back of the picture to the frame, so the picture is airtight and will stay dust-free.

Glycerin

Foliage, such as peony, oak, and beech leaves, will be more supple and usable if treated with glycerin. Glycerin preserves foliage so it will last indefinitely. Before mid-August, gather all foliage to be treated because it will still be tender then.

A solution of one part glycerin and two parts hot water should be mixed in a jar. Shake well. Scrape or pound the ends of the young branches, and place in two to three inches of the solution. Let stand for one to two weeks; much of the solution will be absorbed. The leaves should feel pliable and change colors to dark greens or soft shades of brown and rust.

Include the glycerinized foliage in dried arrangements and fresh floral arrangements; water will not damage the material.

The glycerin solution may be used repeatedly. Keep it stored in a tightly covered jar.

Dried arrangements

Dried plants can be added to both formal and casual arrangements. If flower and leaf stems are short, lengthen them with florist's tape and wire. Combine the blooms with glycerinized foliage in an arrangement in a container filled with florist's foam.

Insert foliage first, using it as a guide for height and outline. Place larger and darker flowers in the lower center section. Fill in the arrangement with more flowers, making sure some of them extend be-

low the rim of the container on the outside. Then place your completed creation in a spot out of direct sunlight.

For a carefree touch, try stalks of wheat, milkweed pods, cattail, and several sprays of curved bittersweet in a tall vase. Choose a vase of a neutral hue to bring out the autumn colors in the dried materials. (Soaring stems of pussy willow, which appear early each spring, will last through the year.) This type of arrangement is particularly at home in an entrance hall, in a corner of a room, or beside a fireplace.

If you use branches of bittersweet or mock bittersweet berries, remember that they are poisonous and should be displayed well out of the reach of children or pets.

Lavender pillows

Lavender pillows are simple to make and retain their fragrant scent for several months. Simply remove the lavender flowers from the stalks and combine with powdered orrisroot. Stuff dainty pillows with the mixture. Use the pillows in closets, trunks, or dresser drawers.

Container Gardening

Postage-stamp yards, decks, balconies, and apartments are all prime candidates for container gardening. Many flowering annuals, bulbs, roses, vegetables, and even small fruit trees and shrubs do well in containers.

Think height as well as length when growing plants in pots. This garden planter puts vertical space to good use.

Well-drained soil, sunlight to fit their needs, protection from overly playful breezes, fertilizer, and lots of moisture—container-grown plants have needs similar to most other plants, but you are in charge of how much they receive and when their needs are met. Container plants do have a big advantage over other plants—they're mobile! You can enhance their beauty and charm by mixing and moving them around.

Remember to keep larger plants in the background and flowering varieties in a spot where the light is right. Almost all container plants should be turned occasionally to encourage symmetrical growth.

Remember, though, that strong winds can present a problem. If plants are not properly weighted with sand mixed with the soil or set in heavy containers, breezes can knock them over. Many plants, such as fuchsias, cannot tolerate the drying effects of wind.

Compared with those who can afford to scatter plants with wild abandon, container growers have to use their wits to get the most from less space. For example, think of your outdoor space as having a vertical dimension, as well as a horizontal one.

Try displaying plants one above the other on a wall—in hanging baskets, planters flattened on one side, or pots on shelves. Not only do you take advantage of the entire plant, but you dramatically increase your total growing room, as well.

Chances are there will be a hot spot on your balcony, deck, or terrace that just can't seem to get out of the sun. Sun lovers will thrive there; try brightly tufted geraniums, selected roses, or flowering shrubs. Or, enough kinds of vegetables to make delightful, delicious salads all summer (see below) will grow well in containers, too.

Sun and heat can play some mean tricks, though; without ventilation and adequate watering, the sunny spot can turn into a micro-desert that will dry up even the hardiest plants. Be sure containers are placed on bricks or pieces of wood to aid air circulation, and make sure the soil is well drained. Check the surface of the soil often, and water when it feels dry to the touch. When hot days are the rule, you may need to water your container plants daily.

This patio garden is easier to care for than an in-ground garden. The benefits of potted crops: no digging, less weeding, and limited stooping and bending.

Use containers filled to the brim with bold-blooming, shade-loving bedding plants to add color to areas lacking light.

plants, such as sweet alyssum, lobelia, and dwarf marigolds, about three to five inches apart; taller plants, such as petunias, celosia, and coleus, about four to six inches apart. Keep annuals with a tendency to get leggy, such as petunias and coleus, pinched back.

To get the best bulb blooms, remember good drainage. If the soil is waterlogged, bulbs may rot and succumb to disease.

Whether grown for their evergreen foliage or spectacular blossoms, shrubs can provide instant landscaping for a terrace, patio, backyard, or deck. Be sure to buy them to stay in scale with their containers and surroundings. Extra-tall types, such as lilacs, are too large to thrive for long in containers. However, medium-size, small, and low-growing shrubs, such as deutzia, cinque-foil, or the ever-popular hills-of-snow hydrangea, are ideal.

After you buy the plant, place it in a container as soon as possible. Fill the bottom of the tub with drainage material (broken pot fragments or gravel), and cover with several inches of coarse peat moss. Be sure your soil mix is adequately moistened. If you're using a clay pot, soak it in water first, so dry clay won't pull all the moisture from the soil. If you're planting a bare-root tree or shrub, fill the pot about halfway with soil formed into a little mound. Spread the roots around the mound and cover with additional soil. Then water well.

Roses need six to eight hours of sunlight a day but seem to like partial shade during the midday hours. An inch of peat moss over the drainage material in their containers keeps the soil from filtering downward and possibly obstructing the free flow of water.

For the owner of a deck or balcony, vines are perfect for disguising pillars, poles, and other supports. Or a brick wall, exposed to the searing rays of the sun, can be transformed into a cool bower of gracefully climbing grape, wisteria, honeysuckle, or a spectacular rose, each grown in its own container.

Petunias planted in old watering cans add a whimsical touch to a porch.

Your favorite kinds of plants and the light conditions available can be brought together in a charming compromise. Many trees, shrubs, walls, buildings, and dividers cast restful, dappled shade just right for such sun-sensitive plants as fuchsia, coleus, impatiens, or tuberous begonia. Where deep shade prevails, use the delicate fronds of the various ferns and the trailing vines of ivies.

Sometimes plants can be lifted out of the shade and into window boxes. Combine plants—flowering and foliage—that complement each other. For soil, buy a lightweight potting mix, or make your own with soil, peat moss, and perlite. Cover the bottom of the box with broken clay pot fragments, and add a layer of coarse peat moss or nylon netting. Then fill with soil. A handful of slow-release fertilizer mixed with the soil will keep the plants healthy. Moisten the soil thoroughly and set out the plants. Or put plants in separate pots and set the pots in the box. This way you can change pots as needed or as your whim for a change of scenery occurs.

Annuals grow well in window boxes or a variety of other containers. Buy seedlings or start your own. When grown in pots or raised beds, most annuals will look best if planted close together. Space low edging

A box filled with coleus, euonymus, and fuchsia brightens a north wall.

Rock Gardens

Eroding slopes, inclines too steep to mow, grade changes, a slant from house to walk or driveway—many landscaping problems are solved with a rock garden. To avoid a helter-skelter look, however, be sure to start with a rough sketch of where the rocks and plants will go.

Plants teamed with rocks are often the best answer when a bank has to be held in place against erosion. Also, up-to-date architecture often features the creation of sharp grade changes; when the change is nearly vertical, a low wall may be required. A dry-stone wall (where materials are loosely piled instead of mortared together) may be the answer for a grade change from terrace to street, for example. The resulting planting pockets between the rocks are perfect locations for favorite rock garden plants.

Be prepared. Although the results may have a casual and informal look, rock gardens will take planning and hard work to establish. And not all your effort will be visible. About a third of each large boulder will be hidden in the side of your "hill." But once the work is done, your rock garden will require little care, and you'll be able to admire it for years.

Careful planning is the essential first step in establishing a good rock garden. Before you cut into the bank, you must know what type and size of rock you'll be using. Plot where rocks will go and where you want interesting undulations in the slope. Plan, too, where major plantings will be.

Just two or three huge boulders are sufficient for a large rock garden. ("Huge" means about three feet in width, length, diameter, or all three.) If the boulders are being

Hardy native plants and succulents, including cacti, transformed this arid, rocky hillside into a colorful oasis.

hauled in from the countryside or a nursery, have them dropped as close as possible to their assigned location in the garden. This will simplify the backbreaking job of moving the heavy boulders.

Best rocks are those that look at home in your setting—those naturally found in your area or some that harmonize with rocks used in your house or patio paving. All the rocks should be of the same general kind, rather than a geologic collection. Weathered rocks are preferred.

Lightweight porous rocks, such as limestone, are ideal. They absorb moisture and act as a buffer during dry spells. Nonporous rocks, such as granite, can cause rapid drying of surrounding soil because they don't absorb moisture. Avoid novelty rocks that call attention to themselves and outshine the plants. Also, avoid all soft and scaly rocks, shale, and unweathered sandstone. For a small area, avoid heavy labor by using easy-to-handle synthetic and volcanic rock.

For the best effect, try to keep the design as informal as possible. The rocks themselves should look as if they were embedded there a century ago, and the plants as if they volunteered to grow without any assistance from a gardener. Vary shapes and sizes of stones and avoid geometric arrangements.

When the major boulders are in place, fill the voids between them with soil mix. Start with a base of garden loam and make it more absorbent by adding perlite, vermiculite, or peat moss—about one-fourth of the volume. Rich soil isn't necessary and may even make the dwarf plants grow too big for their assigned places.

Plants for your garden can include annuals, dwarf evergreens, perennials, hardy bulbs, and succulents. For year-round stability and beauty, you'll want a planting of shrubs. Dwarf mugo pine, cotoneaster, and creeping juniper can fill the bill. Perennials, such as artemisia and sedum, also can be part of the permanent plantings. Then blanket the remaining areas between stones with colorful bedding and foliage plants you set out each spring.

For showy color, assign three to a dozen adjoining planting pockets to

A tribe of wild native plants tamed this steep slope in California, giving life to what was once a rocky wasteland.

a dazzling plant, such as red moss phlox. It will soon grow into one bold mass.

To provide a long season of bloom, include pockets of spring-flowering bulbs in your plans. As their foliage dies down in late spring, fill in their spots with bedding annuals. For color in the fall, plant a few cushion mums.

As a rule of thumb in selecting plants, use those that are known to grow well in your neighborhood. This can cut down on replacements.

Cover the soil around plants and stones with mulching material—redwood bark is a good choice. The mulch will keep down weeds. Rock gardens are easily maintained, but they cannot fend for themselves. If weeds do peek through, pull them out by hand. The dwarf plants usually planted in rock gardens don't compete well with weeds.

Tulips, daffodils, and hyacinths help smother this incline with color.

Ground-hugging candytuft, basket-of-gold alyssum, armeria, heather, coralbells, aubrietia, moss phlox, crested iris, and viola form a flower festival.

Putting rocks into place

For a natural effect, embed at least the bottom third of boulders in your rock garden. Slant flat rocks back into the soil to divert water to plant roots. If rocks are placed in a horizontal position, slanted forward, or placed so upper rocks overhang lower, water will run off them instead of soaking in.

Set the rocks into the slope to form a series of small plateaus and planting pockets. A long slope should be handled as a series of ledges. Start construction at the bottom of the slope, and use both large and small stones to avoid the look of even ridges.

Rock walls should not be absolutely vertical; the face should slant back slightly, with bottom stones larger than top. A slant of two inches for every foot in height is sufficient. Form planting pockets by breaking stones at an angle to form V-shaped spaces. Rock walls are built like masonry walls, except mortar is replaced by soil.

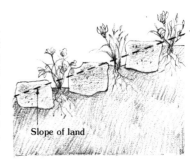

Slope of land

Flowering plants for rock gardens in sun

Alyssum
Evergreen candytuft
Pink saponaria
   (*Saponaria ocymoides*)
Dalmatian bellflower
   (*Campanula portenschlagiana*)
Siebold sedum
Moss phlox
   (*Phlox subulata*)
Thyme
Dwarf columbine
Pink
Creeping veronica

Small rosettes and tufts for sunny exposure

Blue fescue
Dwarf thrift
Dwarf pink
Hen-and-chickens
   (*Sempervivum
   soboliferum*)
Woolly yarrow
Ajuga
Dwarf iris

Plants for shade

Bleeding-heart
Fern
Phlox
Hepatica
Forget-me-not
   (*Myosotis* sp.)
Caladium
Primrose
Tuberous begonia
Bloodroot
   (*Sanguinaria* sp.)
Hosta
Lily-of-the-valley

These start easily from seed sown among rocks

Kenilworth ivy
Bleeding-heart
Blue phlox
Fairy linaria
Iceland poppy
Spanish poppy

Good dwarf annual flowers

Dahlberg daisy
Pygmy marigold

Sanvitalia
Sweet alyssum
Portulaca
Fairy linaria

Spreading plants for large banks

Lavender
Catnip
Cerastium
Moss phlox
Sun rose
   (*Helianthemum* sp.)
Woolly veronica
Hardy verbena
Silver Mound
   artemisia

Annuals suitable for low walls and banks

Dahlberg daisy
Ageratum
Torenia
Fairy linaria
Pygmy marigold
Siberian wallflower
Nierembergia
Lychnis
   (*Haageana* hybrids)

Small bulbs

Crocus, Cloth-of-gold
   (*Crocus angustifolius*)
Grape hyacinth
Chionodoxa (or glory-of-the-snow)
Siberian squill
Galanthus
Kaufmanniana tulip
Eranthis (or winter aconite)

Dwarf shrubs

Alberta spruce
Canby pachistima
Dwarf alpine willow
Dwarf Japanese yew
Garland flower
   (*Daphne cneorum*)
Hypericum
Rhododendron—dwarf
   species and hybrids
Sand myrtle
   (*Leiophyllum* sp.)
Scotch heather
   (*Calluna vulgaris*)
Teucrium

Hints for rock walls

Plan your rock wall carefully and you'll have not only a unique way of displaying plants but also a useful means of preventing erosion.

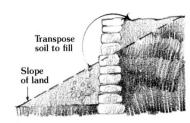

To get more use from a sloping lawn, level it with a retaining wall (above). If the wall is mortared, concentrate on spreading plants set behind it to soften the hard line across the top. Pinks, cerastium, and alyssum are possibilities.

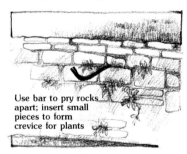

To replace or add plants to an almost vertical wall, spread roots flat, and wrap in wet sphagnum moss. Use a bar to pry rocks apart, and wedge small stones in to make

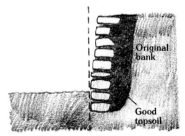

a crevice for plants. Make a downward slanting hole, and slide the wrapped roots into the crevice on a flat trowel, spatula, or pancake turner. Fill in soil around roots.
   Think first of stability when building a new wall. Slant the face back slightly. Ram good soil mix between stones. If possible, plant the perennials as you build.

Sedum, cerastium, and cranesbill fill planting pockets.

This raised-bed garden features herbs and flowers to delight the senses.

Herb Gardens

Herbs display nature's beauty and magic. Yet, they demand little care, spread naturally, and have unique fragrances. Their leaves, stems, blossoms, roots, and stalks are used for the fragrances and flavors you'll love.

Herbs offer a wide range of choices. Whether sweet or sour, subtle or strong, they can be planted formally or informally.

Formal arrangements, or traditional herb plantings, date back a long time. The Roman nobility's idea of luxury was a well-ordered garden gracing the entrances of their homes. A simple, traditional design consists of two three-foot paths crossing at their midpoints. The four square herb beds may be bordered with brick or stones.

Another popular design is the wagon wheel. Bricks or stones are sunk into the ground to form the "spokes" and "rim." Herbs are planted in the wedge segments.

Appearance is important in the traditional herb garden. Keep the walks trimmed and use mulches to combat weeds and retain moisture.

Informal arrangements, such as a sea of spearmint crowding a lawn or walkway, give a refreshing scent when the mint is trampled underfoot or clipped with the lawn mower. Creeping thyme and chamomile offer the same results.

Plant a small garden near your kitchen door. A seven-by-12-foot plot can accommodate as many as ten varieties of herbs. The spot should be in full sun and the soil well drained. Plant your favorites, such as chives, thyme, sage, parsley, basil, rosemary, and mint.

Or, plant a triangle garden. If the sides are about 14 feet long the garden can hold six or seven different

An ornamental bee skep sits amidst a potpourri of herbs.

Chives, parsley, and mint add spice to annuals outside a window.

kinds of herbs. Plant taller mints at the back of the garden. Next, four or five sage plants, then equal amounts of parsley and summer savory. Set chives along the front leg of the triangle and a plant or two of thyme in the corners.

Plant annual cooking herbs among your vegetables. However, plant perennials along the edges of your vegetable garden so you can till it each year. Grow parsley and basil as a border around the vegetables. Sow dill and coriander between tomatoes, cabbage, and broccoli. Herbs often distract or repel pests from your vegetables.

Herbs in containers are handy if you are short on space. Push flue tiles into the ground to make attractive planters and keep the herbs in bounds. Or set out plants in individual clay pots. Indoors, place potted herbs in a sunny window receiving four to six hours of light each day, or grow them under artificial lights. Mist plants occasionally and water regularly.

Use herbs fresh in salads or brew them in teas. Or dry them for fall arrangements, potpourris, or sachets. Several herbs can be frozen. Tie tarragon, chives, parsley, dill foliage, and basil in bunches; then blanch or steam for a minute. Cool, seal in plastic bags, and freeze.

Plant a variety of mints, lemon verbena, balm, thyme, sage, comfrey, and chamomile for traditional teas. Making herbal tea is simple. Use one tablespoon of fresh leaves (or one teaspoon of dried leaves) for each cup of water. Pour boiling water over the leaves, and cover the teapot to let it steep. After three to five minutes, strain and serve.

Potpourris are fragrant blends of dried flowers and spices. To make one, you will need many dried rose petals and a mix of dried garden herbs. Herbs to consider include sage, lemon verbena, rosemary, rose geranium, thyme, mint, basil, chamomile, and caraway. From your spice rack, add cinnamon, allspice, mace, cloves, or nutmeg. Orrisroot is a scent preservative that must be added and can be purchased at most pharmacies. Cure the potpourri in a covered container for five to six weeks, stirring it every few days.

Though it has the look of an informal mixture of fragrant and culinary herbs, this garden was carefully planned.

Shady Gardens

Cool shady spots—so welcome on blistering days—are gardening challenges. Light is a requirement for any plant, but some can get by on less than others. Try the shade-loving plants described on these pages in your low-light areas.

Mayapple, epimedium, shooting-star, fern, bleeding-heart, and hosta enliven this shady spot at the foot of two trees.

Many plants tolerate shade but bloom sparingly without more sun. Others prefer shade and won't grow or bloom well in full sun. You have many plants to choose from for non-sunny spots.

Shade is created in many ways—a nearby apartment house, the spot between the garage and house, a patio on the north side. You can create lush settings for protected patios or decks by filling adjacent planting areas with shade plants or massing potted plants. If you are willing to rotate container-grown plants into the sun for a few hours each day, your choices are almost limitless.

Suggestions here feature plants that tolerate shade permanently. Most of these plants get only indirect light, but this is great for ferns and for ivies draping the walls. Potted plants could include a pink camellia, blue lobelia, fatsia, caladium, and impatiens.

If you have a shaded front walk, extend a special welcome by bordering it with flowers. Combine alyssum and fibrous begonias for a stunning white-on-white effect. Plants soon will grow to good size if planted in loose, rich soil and fed lightly each month.

For a narrow space at the side of a house, planting beds and planters in the paving will make room for several plants. Try including fibrous begonias, cyclamen, ivy, privet hedge, ferns, and a Japanese maple. Use container-grown plants to give the area color.

A shady border in spring can feature the fascinating early growth of ferns; they uncurl! Mix them with arched spikes of bleeding-heart and the bright colors of bulbs. A low mound of wild ginger will form a compact carpet. Large leaves of hosta will provide dramatic contrast to the surrounding lacy foliage.

You'll find advantages to developing a restful haven of plants in that shady stretch or corner. It's far more pleasant to tend to a garden out of the blazing sun. And you may find yourself with fewer gardening chores: plants in the shade require less water, and their flowers almost always last longer.

Your plant choices are many. Shade-loving plants can be found among annuals, hardy perennials, hardy bulbs, tender bulbs, ground covers, vines, evergreens, deciduous flowering shrubs, and small trees.

Perennials for shade. For a refreshing lift year after year, plant several of these perennials.

• Astilbe, sometimes called false spirea, has fern-like leaves and spires of white, pink, or red fluffy flowers on two- to three-foot plants.

• Bee balm is a fragrant plant. The scarlet, lavender, pink, or white blooms appear in late summer.

• Bishop's weed or goutweed (*Aegopodium podagraria*) makes a delightful ground cover when planted with ferns and hostas. It's a vigorous creeping perennial and should be contained. The variegated type is generally the best to plant because the green-leaved variety is more invasive.

• Bleeding-heart—with its pink, heart-shaped flowers—flourishes in spring. The foliage dies down in summer. Everblooming, dwarf varieties are available, also.

• Carpet bugle, ajuga, and bugleweed—all are names for the ground cover *Ajuga reptans*. Its six-inch-high spikes of blue flowers are showy in the spring.

• *Helleborus niger,* or Christmas rose, isn't really a rose, but it's a choice plant that has beautiful flowers at a surprising time of the year. Its leaves are large (ten inches across), evergreen, and divided like fingers. The time to plant is early spring or early autumn. Choose a protected place shaded in summer but with winter sun. Soil should be deeply prepared, with humus worked into it. Water well all year. Similar, but spring-blooming, is the *Helleborus orientalis,* or lenten rose.

• Columbine has airy blossoms that come in white, yellow, pink, red, or blue. The plants grow up to three feet tall.

• Coralbells have tiny pink bells on two-foot stems. The plant is decorative even when not in bloom because of its neat tufts of leaves.

• Hostas have leaves varying from thumbnail to platter size and from heavily quilted to glossy smooth—depending on the variety. These elegant yet hardy plants are best known for their leaves, but send up splendid spikes of white or blue flowers late in the growing season.

• Primroses merit a spot in the shady garden. There are many types. All sport rich, green foliage—crinkled or sometimes ruffled—and two-tone flower blendings of red, yellow, pink, white, and purple.

Make easy-care impatiens the backbone of your shady garden. They'll quickly color even the dullest spot in a yard.

Other shade-loving perennials include hardy ageratum, anchusa, gentian, globeflower, jacob's-ladder, leadwort, lobelia, lungwort, and meadowsweet.

Annuals for shade. For variety, select different annuals each year. They come in a wide assortment of bloom and foliage colors.

• Coleus plants are pretty from the moment they are set out. They are available at just about every garden center.

• Impatiens' blossoms are small, but their effect is great because of their prolific blooming habit. The mounds of glossy green foliage are all but covered with evenly spaced flowers that range through shades of red, orange, pink, and purple to the purest of whites.

Other favorite annuals that thrive in less-than-sunny spots include begonias, calliopsis, cynoglossum, mignonette, and torenia.

Wildflowers also are good candidates to add color to shady spots.

Desert Gardens

Lots of heat and little water may seem to be certain disaster for a garden, but careful selection of plants that love such desert-like conditions can mean an exotic view instead of a barren wasteland.

Combine cactus and other succulents with hardy annuals and perennials tolerant of dry soils. You'll have an exquisite arrangement of fleshy foliage and colorful blooms.

Cactus and other succulents have long been popular among plant collectors and hobbyists for indoor and greenhouse gardening. Now enthusiasts are finding those plants suitable for outdoor use, too. Especially in the Southwest, where the climate is favorable for growing most succulents, these plants will provide beauty and striking looks year-round.

Winter care. In cold climates, tender types can be placed in the garden during summers, in either sun or partial shade. Before frosts come, however, these plants must be brought indoors to a well-lighted window. Or plant them directly in the soil and, in the fall, snap off the offsets to make houseplants. After the offsets have roots, reduce water. Two waterings per month are all that is needed.

Culture. In general, cactus and other succulents require a medium-rich, well-drained soil and as much sunlight as possible. Rock gardens and rock walls are good locations for many succulents.

For once, rocky ground or a slope is a gardening advantage; otherwise, mix in sizable amounts of sand and pebbles to get the soil to drain more quickly. Feed with a high phosphorus fertilizer once a year—in early spring when new growth begins. Provide iron if plants yellow. Water only when weather produces drought-like conditions.

Low-maintenance flower beds and pathways nearly eliminate lawn care in this desert setting in New Mexico.

The wide variety of plants in this group means you can find a cactus or other succulent compatible with your climate, landscape, and other plantings. Besides the familiar spike and barrel shapes covered with spines, there are many shrubs and ground covers.

Pick a plant. Best-known cold-hardy kinds that survive winter temperatures in the North are sedums and sempervivums.

Sedums (sometimes called stonecrop and live-forever) come in both trailing and upright varieties.

Some are evergreen; others, deciduous. Flowers, although they are not the main attraction of these plants, are pretty.

Trailing sedums are often planted in crevices in rock walls or used as a ground cover. Upright sorts can be used to edge perennial borders. All sedums propagate easily; leafy stems produce roots when placed in moist soil.

Sempervivums (often called hen-and-chickens) are rosette in form and evergreen in foliage. As big rosettes mature, they send up flower stalks, then die; but many small plants carry on.

A more striking succulent is the vertical *Aloe striata* with its smooth-edged, spear-like leaves. The orange to red blooms are long lasting.

Aloe brevifolia is a spiny, well-shaped specimen. It has a cluster of thick, sharp leaves that sends out flower stalks 20 inches high with red flowers throughout the year.

Although fewer cactus thrive in cooler zones, the flat, round *Opuntia fragilis* is one of the hardier cactus and will survive temperature extremes through Zone 4.

This arboretum of succulents and native plants will inspire all gardeners.

Use plants indigenous to your area.

Yarrow, red-hot-poker, hollyhock, and penstemon fill this courtyard.

Dazzling fillers

Check with a local nursery for the cactus and other succulents best suited for your area. Then fill in between with the annuals and perennials listed below.

Perennials
Baby's-breath
Baptisia
Butterfly weed
Coreopsis
Felicia
Flax
Gaillardia
Heath aster
  (*Aster ericoides*)
Liatris
Lychnis
Phlox
  (*Phlox subulata*)
Rock cress
  (*Arabis* sp.)
Rudbeckia
Spurge
Yarrow
Yucca

Annuals
Amaranth
Ammobium
Arctotis
Aster
Browallia
Celosia
Cleome
Cornflower
Cosmos
Dusty-miller
Feverfew
Four-o'clock
Gaillardia
Gypsophila
Ice plant
Poppy
Portulaca
Rudbeckia
Salvia
Star-of-Texas
  (*Xanthisma texana*)
Sunflower
Zinnia

Water Gardens

Water lilies, lotus, and other aquatics may be legends along the Nile and in the Orient, but you can enjoy them at home, too. They'll grow just as well in a watertight tub on your patio or small pool in your yard. Or, better yet, build your own backyard pond—complete with aquatic animals that will add color and entertainment.

Water, nature's most sensuous element, is basic to the creation of a truly tranquil garden setting. The presence of sparkling water is enchanting in itself. And the wildlife that even a small pond will attract can bring extra pleasure, filling a lazy summer afternoon with lively entertainment. Tropical aquatic plants and bright-colored fish combine with water to create an exotic environment with its own delicate beauty.

Any watertight container can be a garden pool. A wooden tub or half barrel can be set above or into the ground. Or build an in-ground pond using cement, preformed plastic or fiberglass pools, or a PVC (polyvinyl chloride) pool liner.

If desired, to give the effect of a musical, natural spring, combine a dripstone with an underground water line. The dripstone should extend far enough forward to form a sound chamber. Water lilies dislike running water, so use other plants around the pool edges.

Exquisite water plants grow in soil-filled containers submerged in water. If you're using a single large plant in a big tub, plant directly in the bottom of the container and fill tub with water.

At planting time, fill the container with garden loam. Incorporate slow-release fertilizer at the rate suggested on the package. Add clay to the mix for lotus.

Plant hardy water lilies in late spring. Press soil firmly about tuber, so crown of plant is above the soil line. Top the soil with a layer of sand. The surface of the sand should be six to eight inches below the surface of the water. In late fall, store hardy water lily tubers in a cool spot in the basement. Treated this way, your hardy water lilies should live for many years.

If you try tropical water lilies, treat them as annuals, replacing them every year. Tropical lilies give you the choice of using different varieties from year to year, changing the effect they have on your pond. For example, some tropical types bloom during the day and others at night.

Water lilies flourish in a cement-lined pool and will add an exotic dimension to any water garden.

Lotus tubers are planted horizontally, so the growing tip extends above the soil. Cover the rest of the tuber with a shallow layer of soil and a sprinkling of sand. Cover the growing tip with two to four inches of water. After the plant becomes established, increase water to ten inches. To reuse the plants next year, be sure to dig up the tubers in late fall and store them in a cool basement over the winter.

Water creatures. Colorful fish and other aquatic inhabitants will add to your pond's fascination. They also help control insects and algae growth naturally by feeding on them. Wastes of water animals provide organic fertilizer for the pool's plants.

Before adding any aquatic life to your pool, let the water rest for a week so the chlorine disperses. The smaller your pond, the fewer fish you should stock; a good rule of thumb is one fish per every two square feet of surface area. To help acclimate fish, float them for 30 minutes in your pond in the plastic bag you bring them home in. Choose a variety of colorful goldfish, including calicoes, comets, black moors, and fantails. Golden orfe or Japanese koi will add lively contrast. These close cousins in the carp family do best in a pool at least three feet deep.

Welcome snails, turtles, and frogs, too, if they come calling. They're harmless to plants.

Depending on the area you live in and depth of your pool, you may need to drain it during winter. Or, if not, you may need to remove the fish. Check with your local pool and fish suppliers for directions.

Constructing a water garden. If you think building a backyard water garden is for experts only, you're mistaken. The step-by-step illustrations (right) show that creating your own pond is well within your do-it-yourself abilities.

The classical water gardens you see in most formal settings are made of hand-packed concrete. Now there are simpler ways to install a water garden by using preformed plastic or fiberglass pool shapes or polyvinyl chloride (PVC) liners that mold to the excavated site's shape.

Before digging in, choose your site carefully. It should be sunny for at least five hours a day and handy to a garden hose. Simple shapes are best for small spaces. Do not build a pool that measures less than 40 square feet. A smaller body of water collects more heat and light, creating the perfect environment for algae.

Make your pool at least 18 inches deep, a comfortable depth for both plants and most fish. You'll need to provide raised patches of soil for water plants. You can either create different levels of underwater terraces or set pots of plants on bricks stacked to the appropriate height for the plant. Pots are easiest for small ponds.

The instructions at right will guide you through each step of the building process. For simplicity's sake, this free-form pond uses a PVC liner.

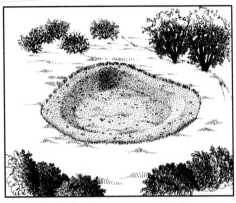

1. *Dig the hollow to the desired size and shape. Use a pond shape that will blend with your yard. Allow for a 3-inch layer of sand or gravel under the lining. The final water depth should be at least 18 inches for plants and most fish to cohabit.*

2. *Check that there are no sharp objects that could pierce the PVC lining. Line the hollow with sand or gravel. This will provide an even bed for the lining. Edge the pond with bricks.*

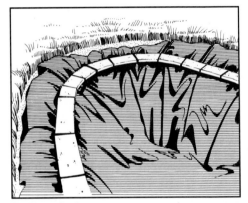

3. *Place the lining in position, making sure it is not under any tension. Allow about 12 inches extra lining all around. Gather the edges and fold them under the edging bricks.*

4. *Position pots of water plants at their proper heights. Fill the pond with water; allow the liner to settle for one week. The settling will create a gap between the brick edging and the lawn; fill the gap with gravel.*

5. *Cover the gravel edging with cement. Check that the edge of the PVC lining is not showing through under the bricks. Slope the cement surface slightly inward for drainage.*

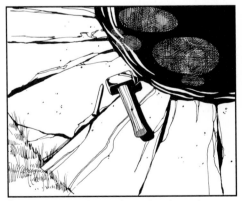

6. *Finish the edge with wedge-shaped stones, such as sandstone or slate, allowing them to overhang the water. Set them so they slope slightly inward. Cement stones in position.*

Fancy Grasses

Swaying fronds of tall, ornamental grasses add graceful elegance to your landscape design. Lofty ones can act as finely textured screens, and short ones fill bare spots in a flower border or edge a walk. Many do double duty. Dried, they add a wispy look to winter bouquets for any room in the house.

Ornamental grasses reduce yard work—plus add a mark of distinction with a variety of shapes, sizes, and textures.

Gardening with ornamental grasses may be just the touch needed to give your backyard a finished look and make it different from others in the neighborhood.

Fancy grasses will turn any sunny spot into a miniature wild prairie. Their graceful foliage and flower plumes will add special beauty to any yard. They're durable and drought tolerant, too, keeping maintenance to a minimum. At the same time, you can be growing your own material for a dried arrangement to put on a mantel, buffet, or table.

For greatest effect, clump two or more plants of one species near a similar-size group of another. Repeat these clumps periodically at intervals for balance and for a variety of textures.

Or, if your entry planting needs a mark of distinction, try the wispy filler *Helictotrichon sempervirens* or blue oats. Its arching foliage and unusual color make it an excellent choice for front-of-the-border placement. Team it with almost any combination of annual or perennial flowers. It makes a cheery sidewalk edging, too.

Fancy grasses can combine to form a dramatic grouping. The tasseled *Pennisetum setaceum* or annual fountain grass offers an unusual look. Tall *Spartina pectinata,* often called cordgrass, makes a good plant for the back of a grouping. And a good choice for edges are tufts of bluish sheep fescue or *Festuca ovina.*

Sheep fescue by itself can also make a wonderfully work-free ground cover. The silvery blue tufts have ornamental value—with practicality as a bonus. The ten-inch wiry clumps grow in sun or shade equally well but don't tolerate traffic with the resilience of many other ground covers. Sheep fescue is a good choice in Zone 3 southward.

Towers of *Miscanthus sinensis,* a winter-hardy perennial grass, will provide eye-level privacy for loungers and sunbathers on a patio. It grows up to six feet high. A variegated form of this species, commonly called zebra grass, is also available for use in the garden.

Another perennial ornamental grass to consider is *Erianthus ravennae,* or plume grass. It sends up 12-foot-high plumes from three-foot plants. Bamboo-like *Arundo donax* (also called giant reed) grows six to eight feet tall. It is hardy in the South and makes a good potted plant in the North, if you have a suitable spot to winter it indoors. *Carex morrowii 'variegata,'* a sedge, is another perennial possibility; it grows only a foot high and has striped foliage.

Don't overlook the outstanding grasses that can be grown annually from seeds. Try bold pampas grass (*Cortaderia*)—a half-hardy perennial usually grown as an annual. Its silky plumes wave ten feet high. Cut and dry them to add a natural, comfortable look to a corner indoors where live foliage plants don't survive because of low light. Pampas grass seems to fall in and out of favor with interior designers; no matter, this natural material is inexpensive. Use it the way you want with your interior decor.

Outdoors, you can add a decorator's touch with the popular edging plant, liriope. Blooming in summer, its flowers resemble grape hyacinth. This ground cover is fine for the shade. Set the young plants nine ·inches apart in a spot protected from foot traffic. Liriope is a good choice in Zone 5 and any place south (see map, pages 46 and 47).

Or try quaking grass (*Briza*). It forms bushy plants just a foot tall and has cone-shaped seed heads that tremble in a breeze. For something different, plant job's-tears (*Coix lacryma-jobi*). It sets pearly-white seeds that can be dried and strung for beads. Other annuals that are good for long-lasting mixed bouquets are foxtail millet (*Setaria italica*), cloud grass (*Agrostis nebulosa*), and squirreltail grass (*Hordeum jubatum*).

Seldom-used ornamental grasses deserve attention as dramatic landscape accents—and for other uses limited only by the imagination. However, take care to keep ornamental grasses under control. Some self-seed, so pick seed heads when mature to keep plants confined.

*A pot makes a great home for small species like blue fescue (*Festuca ovina glauca*) and quaking grass (*Briza media*).*

*Surround daylilies with golden variegated hakonechloa (*Hakonechloa macra aureola*) for blooms among blades.*

Attract Wildlife to Your Garden

Plant a special garden and soon special friends will come calling. A wildlife garden brings a new dimension to your backyard. The trees and shrubs that attract birds and furry little animals are lovely, too.

Entice wildlife with three irresistible lures: food, water, and shelter. All are plentiful in this welcoming setting.

When you have a wildlife garden, you're a part of the soothing but always busy world of nature. Keep your bird feeder supplied with seeds in the winter and add bits of string in the spring and you'll have visitors darting in and out of the yard. But when you have the plants they love, too, they are more likely to set up housekeeping or call even more often. If you can boast wildlife visitors, the sweet scent of flowers, and the beauty of berried trees and shrubs, you'll have the most pleasing, alive garden ever.

But the advantages don't stop with the aesthetics. Consider birds, for example. As natural controllers of insects, their ability is unequaled. Fledglings eat more than double their own weight in insects daily during summer months. A single flicker can consume thousands of ants a day.

Four basic needs are shared by birds and other wildlife: food, water, shelter from weather and enemies, and a safe home.

A small pond in an open area next to trees and shrubs (above), and set among rock garden plants, makes a perfect birdbath. An inverted lid of a garbage can or a large waterproof saucer sunk in the ground can serve equally well as an inviting watering and bathing place for birds.

If you have dogs or cats, you'll soon find out that wildlife view them as marauders. But they often can coexist with some help from you. When pets share the same yard with wild visitors, be careful to plant "escape" trees close to birdbaths, and set feeders away from thick bushes where your usually docile tabby can hide in ambush.

Some wildlife get a bit greedy, to the extent that they can drive away other visitors. Squirrels, for example, appreciate the seeds set out for birds. To keep squirrels welcome, provide ground-level feeders for them and swinging or pole-supported feeders for birds. Without this plan, squirrels will raid the bird feeders. If you're trying to grow vegetables, screen the crops with wire-mesh and lath boxes or cages to keep rabbits and squirrels at bay.

A formal birdbath can become a watering stop for squirrels, too.

Berries for birds

Bird-pleasing berries are borne by colorful trees and shrubs that make charming additions to your yard. Many of these heavily fruiting trees and shrubs bloom beautifully in the spring or early summer, so you get a colorful bonus in addition to the birds that come to dine later.

When planning your landscape to attract birds, include shrubs such as flowering quince, abelia, boxwood, holly, privet, mock orange, yew, and rugosa rose. Plant trees such as horse chestnut, serviceberry, redbud, eastern wahoo (*Euonymus atropurpurea*), hawthorn, and sweet gum. For bird fare during summer months, you might also include Virginia creeper, chokeberry, barberry, dogwood, honeysuckle, hackberry, red mulberry (*Morus rubra*), and elderberry.

Huckleberry fruits (*Gaylussacia sp.*) are choice food for robins, sapsuckers, waxwings, and bluebirds. The fruits appear in abundance on tall handsome plants that form an excellent privacy screen for outdoor living areas. With little or no care, they'll give you a perennial supply of food for your fine-feathered visitors.

Perhaps the most brilliant fruit in late summer (and into the winter months) is produced by the mountain ash. It also has handsome foliage and is well suited to small properties.

This ash does best when it receives full sun. Its red-orange fruit clusters will attract robins, bluebirds, cedar waxwings, finches, grosbeaks, grouse, Baltimore orioles, woodpeckers, and catbirds.

Annual and perennial flowers can provide food throughout the summer and fall. The seeds of sunflowers, marigolds, and zinnias are popular with the birds. Check with local nurseries, bird societies, and the county extension office for regional advice.

If you really appreciate birds, provide food supplies for the hardy ones spending the winter in your area. They'll go for such fruiting plants as bittersweet, hawthorn, euonymus, holly, juniper, buckthorn, sumac, and hemlock.

To prevent birds from damaging those fruits you're going to use, protect trees with netting. Also, plant berried shrubs to give birds a free meal. Your fruit trees won't look quite so alluring. Tempt birds away from strawberries, blackberries, raspberries, and cherries by dotting mulberry, serviceberry, and elderberries around your yard. Virginia creeper could divert them from grapes. You'll probably suffer some losses, but these other attractions should reduce them. Keep feeder trays filled with an assortment of seeds, grains, nuts, and some grit, such as sand or crushed shells. A separate hanging of suet will keep bird traffic brisk. Place such treats well away from your garden.

Birds vary in their preferences. Although many birds like to augment their insect diets with your vegetables, berries, and other fruits, wrens are, first and foremost, insect eaters. They have a preference for leafhoppers, plant lice, scale insects, whiteflies, and even the tiniest insect eggs. Install a wren house in your yard to encourage a pair to set up housekeeping in the area.

A baby robin perches, readying to test its wings.

Bright blossoms, such as this strawflower, will attract beautiful butterflies, which add flittering color to your yard.

Planning a "Wild" Garden

In nature, plants that grow in a certain area result from a network of causes—the climate, soil, topography, and more. The plants will attract certain birds and animals. In your yard, you are the one to evaluate the conditions, select the plants, and place them to attract little creatures to your "wild" garden.

Planning a garden with wildlife in mind differs from most other kinds of landscaping because all the trees and shrubs have two purposes. They either provide food in the form of fruit, seeds, or berries, or are exceptionally well suited as nesting sites or shelter. Of course, many of the fruiting species are ornamental at flowering time, too, so you aren't completely sacrificing beauty in the bargain.

If you stagger the planting over several years, put the trees in the ground the first season. They grow slowly and should be given priority in your garden.

As a rule, shrubs give the effect you want sooner than trees. Put them in the planting plan the first season, if budget permits, or at least by the second season. For example, you might start by planting a *Symphoricarpos albus* (or snowberry) in the spring. You'll find it a useful shrub because it's small and grows in partial shade. The snowberry's white, grape-like fruits are a good lure for jays, grosbeaks, juncos, and finches. Later, you might add a mountain ash tree. It grows to medium size and is excellent for city lots.

Cotoneasters come in many sizes and shapes. Their fruits are appreciated by many kinds of birds, including robins and waxwings. The tall, spreading varieties of cotoneasters make a tight green hedge; medium sizes are for foundation plantings; and low, spreading forms are great for naturalizing.

While waiting for plants to mature, set out feeders and provide water. In fact, many wildlife enthusiasts continue to provide food even after their trees and shrubs are mature. One reason is that they have a better opportunity to view visiting birds and animals at a well-placed feeder. Also, even a carefully planned set of trees and shrubs won't produce food crops constantly. Supplemental feeding is in order.

Many specialists feed birds all year, believing that summer birds will maintain their high ratio of animal (insect) food versus plant food, regardless of ready availability. Feeder food draws flocks, and the birds complete their meals with a dessert of garden insects.

On the plan (opposite), you'll notice brush and rock piles. Devices such as these are valuable for shelter. Bolster this effect by relaxing a little when cleaning your garden. Don't rake under dense stands of shrubs and trees. A small length of rotting log could harbor a friendly toad. During the night, toads eat just about any pest that moves—cutworms, slugs, and potato beetles. One toad can devour up to 15,000 insects in a garden season. Provide a shallow container of water to encourage toads to remain in your garden.

Also include an open area, like the grassy section in the plan. Robins and other birds find grass a gold mine of worms after a summer rain. You will also want to keep an area open for your own enjoyment and to better see your wildlife visitors.

KEY for right page

1. **Flowering dogwood** *is a large shrub or small tree with fruit favored by 36 species of birds. The plant's flowers are ornamental. Native on East Coast and in the South; use red-osier dogwood elsewhere.*

2. **Highbush cranberry viburnum** *is a tall, upright shrub with showy white flowers and glossy red fruit. It grows quickly bearing fruit the second year.*

3. **White oak,** *a grand shade tree that produces acorns enjoyed by squirrels, blue jays, thrashers, and flickers, is a good nest site.*

4. **Elderberries** *are decorative small trees that produce fruit tasty in pies and jams. The 30 species of birds that like elderberries will give you competition on the harvesting.*

5. **Wild species** *of grapes will attract birds when fruit is ripe. Other vines providing cover are bittersweet and Virginia creeper.*

6. **Brush piles** *of twigs and small limbs provide protection from predators, as well as nest sites. When set near watering/bathing spots, birds and small animals can use the shelter as a place to escape when frightened.*

7. **Winterberry** *attracts 22 species of birds, along with some animals. These big shrubs often serve as nest sites, too.*

8. **White pines** *are large trees that work well as winter windbreaks, screens, and nest sites. Cardinals, chickadees, and crossbills are just a few of the species of birds that use white pine seeds for food.*

9. **Blackberries** *permitted to naturalize into a thorny tangle become nest sites and escape areas. Berries are popular as food for birds.*

10. **A shallow pool** *of water is essential for birds and other animals. Unless you want fish, make the pool only a few inches deep, with a rough-finished or rocky surface. Sweep it out often and add fresh water, or install a recirculating pump.*

11. **A rock pile** *becomes protection for toads and other tiny creatures.*

12. **Crab apples** *are small, ornamental trees that produce bird-pleasing fruits. Don't get one of the sterile varieties, such as Spring Snow. They don't set fruits.*

13. **Hawthorn** *is a petite, domed tree with clustered flowers and red fruits. It provides choice sites for nests.*

14. **Viburnum or nannyberry** *attracts blue jays, robins, bluebirds, waxwings, and many other songbirds.*

15. **Honeysuckle**—*a tall variety, not a dwarf—does well along a fence. It will take shade of the surrounding trees and shrubs.*

16. **Red maples** *are dense trees with tops for nesting but serve as only a fair food source for birds.*

17. **A beech tree** *supplies nest sites. Big birds, such as flickers, grosbeaks, and woodpeckers, like the nuts; squirrels love them, also.*

18. **Autumn olive elaeagnus** *is good for shelter, escape, and food. Let it grow in shrub form; do not prune heavily.*

19. **Sumac,** *an interesting tall shrub that produces conical clusters of red fruits, pleases 17 birds. Plants sucker freely and can become a pest.*

20. **White spruce** *is a native evergreen that gives good winter cover.*

Consider Your Climate

With the information from the temperature zone map at right, you can learn the approximate range of minimum temperatures in all parts of the country, and more particularly in your area. Use this map to help choose the right plants for your garden.

The climate in your area is a mixture of many different weather patterns: sun, snow, rain, wind, humidity. To be a good gardener, you should know, on an average, how cold the garden gets in winter, how much rainfall it receives each year, and how hot or dry it becomes in a typical summer. You can obtain this general information from your state agricultural school or your county extension agent. In addition, acquaint yourself with the mini-climates in your own neighborhood, based on such things as wind protection gained from a nearby hill, or humidity and cooling offered by a local lake or river.

Then carry the research further by studying the microclimates that characterize your own plot of ground. Land on the south side of your house is bound to be warmer than a constantly shaded area exposed to cold, northwest winds. An area in the full, hot sun is generally drier than a depression along a drainage route.

Watch how the snow piles up in the garden. Drifts supplying valuable extra water may be caused by the shape of the house or a deflection of wind around a high fence or wall. Study the length of tree shadows in winter and summer and use the information to avoid disappointments. All these findings can help you decide what to plant and where to grow it best.

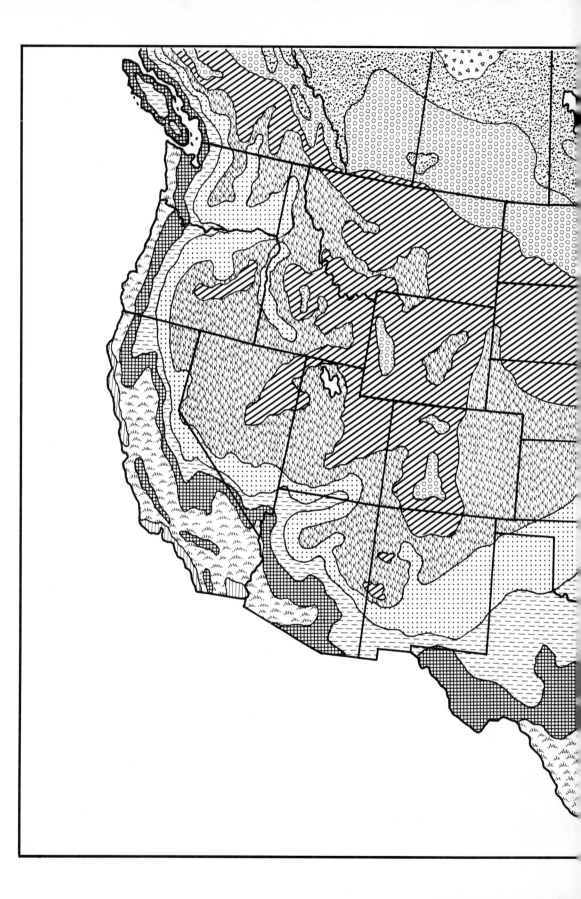

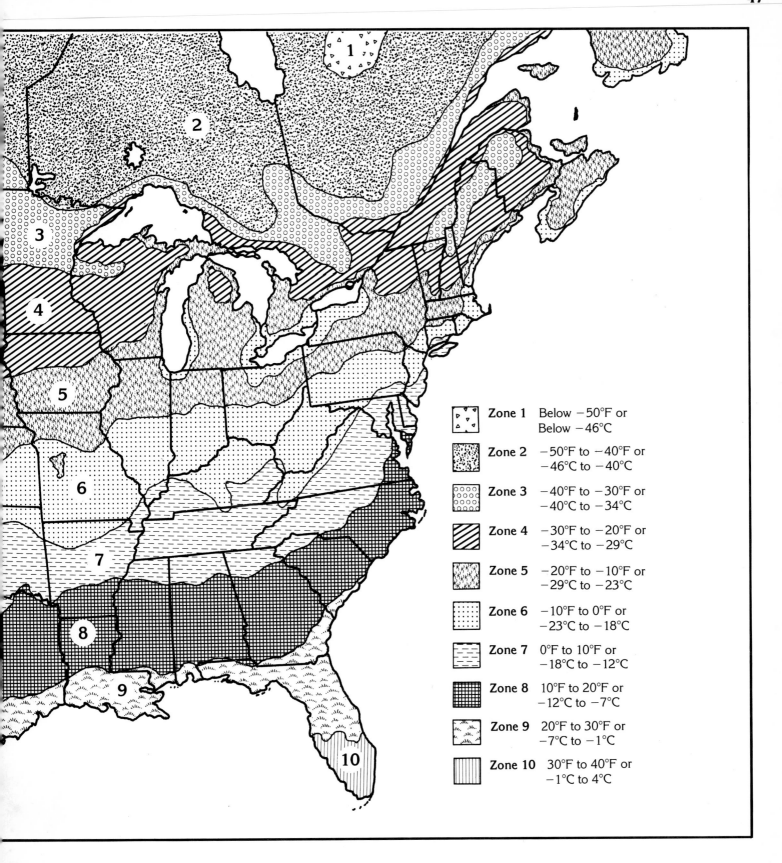

Zone 1 — Below −50°F or Below −46°C

Zone 2 — −50°F to −40°F or −46°C to −40°C

Zone 3 — −40°F to −30°F or −40°C to −34°C

Zone 4 — −30°F to −20°F or −34°C to −29°C

Zone 5 — −20°F to −10°F or −29°C to −23°C

Zone 6 — −10°F to 0°F or −23°C to −18°C

Zone 7 — 0°F to 10°F or −18°C to −12°C

Zone 8 — 10°F to 20°F or −12°C to −7°C

Zone 9 — 20°F to 30°F or −7°C to −1°C

Zone 10 — 30°F to 40°F or −1°C to 4°C

INDEX